WOULD YOU RATHER

BOOK FOR KIDS

Camping & Wildlife Edition

Fun, Silly , Challenging and Thought-Provoking
Questions for Kids, Teens and the Whole Family

Jake Jokester

How to Play
~The Rules~

- You need at least 2 players to play.

- Choose who will go first. The first player chooses a question for the next player (player 2) to answer.

- Player 2 chooses one answer out of the 2 options

You cannot answer "both" or neither".

Optional rule: the answering player has to explain why they made the choice that they made.

- The player who answered the last question becomes the next asker. If there are more than 2 players, you can either pick any person to answer the next question or you can just ask the person next to you, going around in a circle.

Most important rule: Laugh, smile and have lots of fun!

Thanks for getting our book!

If you enjoy using it and it gives you lots of laughs and fun moments, we would appreciate your review on Amazon. Just head on over to this book's Amazon page and click "Write a customer review".

We read each and every one of them.

go trekking barefoot

OR

swim with your clothes on?

eat twinkies for dessert

OR

eat trail mix for dessert?

Would You Rather...

camp for a whole year

never go camping at all?

find a buried treasure

find the ruins of a lost civilizaton
that will make you famous?

Would You Rather...

run away with your shirt pulled up over your head when attacked by bees to prevent your face from the stings

jump in the nearby shallow muddy pond when attacked by bees?

wear an inflatable vest

wear an inflatable donut?

make a raft and go rafting under
the guidance of an expert

OR

fly a drone and take stunning aerial
shots of your surroundings?

eat one apple a day

OR

eat one banana a day?

live in a van

live on a farm?

lose your only pair of shoes
on your camping trip

lose the only pack of food
that you have with you?

roll in the mud

OR

eat a bowl of cooked
bugs for dinner?

be chased by squirrels

OR

be attacked by a
group of rabbits?

find a golden apple

OR

eat a fresh and
delicious apple pie?

go snorkeling

OR

go surfing?

Would You Rather...

go camping in a camper van

OR

go camping and stay in a tent?

have holes in your socks

OR

have to carry rocks
in your pockets?

Would You Rather...

see a wild boar

OR

hear a lion roar?

wear high heels on a 2-week
long camping trip

OR

go barefoot in the snow on
a winter camping trip?

have vanilla on your hot dog

OR

have ketchup on your ice cream?

hear a snapping sound at night

OR

hear a loud growl during the day?

Would You Rather...

go camping in The Alps in France

OR

go camping in Tasmania, Australia?

go camping at a palace

OR

go glamping (glamorous camping) in the Moon?

Would You Rather...

stay indoors and watch TV

OR

stay outdoors and go camping?

go fishing

OR

go hiking?

Would You Rather...

run out of water on a mountain

OR

run out of matches for the fire?

be able to name all
the trees you see

OR

officially have one star
named after you?

Would You Rather...

sing a campfire song

OR

shoot a bow and arrow?

bring your best friend to camping

OR

bring your whole group of
friends for camping?

swim in a lake

hike a mountain?

run around naked in the rain

jump over a fire?

watch the sunrise

OR

watch your favorite TV show?

catch lots of fish under the
guidance of an expert

OR

harvest a large quantity of honey
under the guidance of an expert?

Would You Rather...

play charades

OR

go to a masquerade?

meet a leopard in the forest

OR

meet a leprechaun in the forest?

Would You Rather...

kiss a frog

kiss your grandpa?

have the vision of an owl

have the smelling abilities
of a dog?

Would You Rather...

go on a campsite
scavenger hunt

pick flowers?

spend a day as a cartoon character

spend a day as a baboon?

camp in an igloo

OR

camp in a mud hut?

like to see a beautiful peacock just outside your tent, the first thing when you wake up in the morning

OR

see a group of majestic gazelles just outside your tent, the first thing when you wake up in the morning?

look for wildlife

OR

look for alien life?

be a crocodile

OR

be a lizard?

purr like a cat

OR

growl like a lion?

spend the night in
a 4-star hotel

OR

spend the night camping in
a tent on top of a mountain
with a spectacular view?

Would You Rather...

fight a bear in the woods

OR

fight a snake in the forest?

have a flying tent

OR

have your own boat that
can go underwater?

Would You Rather...

brush your teeth with soap

OR

wash your hair with toothpaste?

pet a scorpion

OR

pet a cobra?

be a dragonfly hovering over lakes

 OR

be a firefly flashing your light
out in forests and fields?

build a huge igloo

 OR

build a tree house?

Would You Rather...

live on an island

OR

live on a mountaintop?

go camping and stargaze
lying on hammock

OR

go camping and play
charades with friends?

Would You Rather...

go and see King Cobra, world's longest venomous snake in the Jungles of Kerala in India

OR

go and see the Black Mamba, the world's deadliest snake in the rainforests of the Democratic Republic of the Congo?

eat cat food

OR

eat dog food?

Would You Rather...

have a bad allergy

OR

have a bad sunburn?

spend all night alone in the woods

OR

all day alone in a classroom?

camp in a tent

OR

camp in an RV?

walk on burning embers

OR

walk over the thin ice of a 3
feet (1,2m) deep puddle?

Would You Rather...

skip school

OR

skip the dentist?

take a mountain motorcycle
and be up for speed

OR

take a mountain bike and
enjoy the view?

Would You Rather...

drink only soda on a
week-long camping trip

 OR

drink only cold water on a
week long camping trip?

have a sleeping bag race

 OR

go on a fast car chase?

Would You Rather...

forget your sleeping bag

 OR

forget your flashlight?

gaze at the stars

 OR

graze on the grass?

Would You Rather...

be able to talk to crickets

OR

to stop the mosquitoes from buzzing and biting you?

catch and collect fireflies in a jar

OR

do bird photography?

have an invisible friend

OR

eat an invisible cake?

see an owl at night

OR

see a bat at night?

Would You Rather...

hear a ghost story

OR

listen to the cicadas?

find gold at the end
of the rainbow

OR

find a burried treasure
chest on an island?

go deep sea diving

go bungee jumping?

be sharp as a pencil

be cool as a mountain stream?

Would You Rather...

camp in a national park

OR

camp in an amusement park?

be stuck in an island
camping alone

OR

be stuck with someone who keeps on
talking about politics the whole time?

Would You Rather...

be an elephant calf in the
savannahs of Africa

OR

be a tiger cub in the mangrove
forests of India?

ride a tiger

OR

ride a bear?

Would You Rather...

go camping during Halloween

OR

go camping during Christmas?

camp next to a Christmas tree

OR

camp next to a palm tree?

be able to talk to birds

OR

be able to talk to fish?

go mountain camping

OR

do seaside camping?

be a seal in sea caves

OR

be a seahorse in coral reefs
in Pacific waters?

eat amazingly delicious
food in the dark

OR

eat canned food but with light?

forget sunscreen

OR

forget bug spray?

listen to a ukulele
at the campfire

OR

listen to hip-hop music
at the campfire?

Would You Rather...

go camping and stay awake late-night listening to ghost stories told by your friends

OR

go camping and wake up early in the morning to go bird watching?

trees could talk

OR

fish could walk?

Would You Rather...

get stung by bees

 OR

get a bad sunburn?

go for a swim at the lake

 OR

stay up late?

Would You Rather...

lay down in a bed of flowers

 OR

lay down in your
own bed at home?

wear flowers in your hair
every day for a year

 OR

eat flowers with your food
once per day for a year?

Would You Rather...

go camping

OR

go on a cruise?

go on a camping trip with a group of your schoolteachers and you being the only student in the group

OR

go on a camping trip with your classmates without any school teachers and without any maps or compasses?

Would You Rather...

have unlimited wifi

OR

have unlimited wisdom?

look like a frog

OR

smell like a skunk?

walk with your feet tied up

OR

sleep with your eyes open?

find a unicorn out in a field

OR

find a fairy in the forest?

Would You Rather...

survive just on chocolate when stranded out in the wild

OR

survive just on canned corn when stranded out in the wild?

have a great compass

OR

have a great sleeping bag?

be slow like a sloth

OR

be fury like a ferret?

see a wolf play with sheep

OR

see a sheep chase a wolf?

Would You Rather...

fly like an eagle

OR

climb like a monkey?

take in a stray cat

OR

take in a stray dog?

Would You Rather...

walk like a penguin to get around

OR

jump like a kangaroo
to get around?

be kept awake all night

OR

sleep for the whole day?

Would You Rather...

own a cow that produced
chocolate milk

OR

own a tree that grows
french fries?

go camping to the 'Grand Canyon
National Park', Arizona in USA

OR

go camping to 'The Isle of
Arran' in Scotland?

camp in spring season

OR

camp in fall (autumn)?

go to watch Tigers in the 'Jim Corbett Tiger Reserve' in India

OR

go camping at the 'Arches National Park', Utah in USA?

have a magic wand

OR

have a magic crystal ball?

scare your fellow campers
with a fake rubber snake

OR

scare your fellow campers by
posing as a ghost growling &
moaning outside of their tents?

Would You Rather...

go 'Whale watching' at
Reykjavik in Iceland

OR

go and see a wild anaconda in the
Amazon river basin in Colombia?

go hiking at night

OR

go to the movies in the morning?

Would You Rather...

have your tent stolen

OR

have your tongue swollen?

have the hands of a kitten

OR

have a hairy wagging tail
of a puppy?

camp at the edge of a cliff

OR

camp under a bridge in the middle of the city?

sleep in the same tent together with a snake

OR

bathe with a bear?

go to see kangaroos in the 'Murramarang National Park' in Australia

go to see ostriches in the 'Waza National Park' in Cameroon (Africa)?

sleep only in a tent

sleep in a sleeping bag?

Would You Rather...

spend a year in the woods

OR

spend a day on a spaceship
in outer space?

explore a mountain cave

OR

explore an underwater cave?

Would You Rather...

go mushroom picking in autumn

 OR

go flower picking in spring?

ride an eagle

 OR

ride a gigantic lion like
Aslan from Narnia?

Would You Rather...

smell a city rat

 OR

smell a wild skunk?

go camping with just your friends

 OR

go camping with family?

live in a hunter's cabin

OR

live in a fisherman's cottage?

be a lion in a cage in a zoo

OR

be a free ant in a jungle?

go camping in cold weather

 OR

go camping in hot weather?

be Superman

 OR

be Spiderman?

Would You Rather...

go camping to the destination of
your choice with your friends

 OR

visit a renowned national
park with your family?

lose your tent

 OR

lose your clothes?

Would You Rather...

eat gravy in the shower

OR

shower in maple syrup?

spend 8 hours hiking

OR

spend 8 hours studying?

do white water rafting

 OR

do dog sledding?

find a fairy in the woods

 OR

a genie in a bottle in the
middle of a desert?

Would You Rather...

have hair as long
as Rapunzel's

OR

have claws as long
as Wolverine's?

help a beaver build his home

OR

help your dad build a fire?

Would You Rather...

go camping in the middle
of fall (autumn)

OR

go camping in the middle
of winter?

make friends with a skunk

OR

become enemies with a hedgehog?

count the stars

OR

count your blessings?

carry medicine that helps
with stomach ache

OR

carry medicine that helps
with diarrhea?

Would You Rather...

get super skinny because you
forgot food for camping

OR

get super tan because
you forgot sunblock?

go camping to the mountains
on horseback

OR

go camping to the mountains
on a camper van?

Would You Rather...

be a fuming bull in a bullfighting
arena charging towards
the matador with rage

OR

be a wild elephant stomping towards
a group of hunters in the jungle?

open a tin can with your mind

OR

melt ice instantly with your breath?

Would You Rather...

be a penguin in Antarctica

 OR

be a peacock in the lush green forests of India?

go glamping (glamorous camping)

 OR

go backpacking?

Would You Rather...

go kayak

go canoe?

get a back rub

get a foot massage?

discover an undiscovered mountain

OR

discover a new species
out in the woods?

get eaten by a bear

OR

get eaten by a crocodile?

kick a hornet's nest

OR

jump into a pit of snakes?

learn how to read tracks

OR

learn how to read minds?

Would You Rather...

go camping and listen to nature, relax and take lots of naps?

 OR

go on a trip to Switzerland?

lay down on the green grass

 OR

make snow angels?

Would You Rather...

run like a rabbit

 OR

slither like a snake?

go camping and
play hide-and-seek

 OR

go camping and play
'Capture the Flag'?

go camping in the
Savannahs of Africa

OR

go camping near the frozen
river in Canada?

carry a swiss knife

OR

carry a flashlight?

Would You Rather...

spend the whole day at
the top of a mountain

OR

spend the whole day
swimming in a lake?

carry a grudge for the whole day

OR

be happy and carry a heavy
backpack for the whole day?

Would You Rather...

have toilet paper stuck on your shoe

OR

have no toilet paper left?

visit Mars

OR

visit the past?

cook for everyone on a camping trip

OR

set up tents for everyone
on a camping trip?

have whiskers

OR

have wings?

Would You Rather...

sleep with bonfire for light

 OR

sleep in total darkness?

make shadow puppets

 OR

play flashlight tag?

have a ten-storey tent

OR

a 10-feet underground lair?

paint rocks

OR

make mud pies?

Would You Rather...

hear a super spooky ghost story

see an actual ghost?

go camping with your parents

go fishing with your grandparents?

Would You Rather...

play hopscotch

OR

eat butterscotch?

dig a hole in the ground
for 5 hours

OR

bring wood for the fire
for 5 hours?

Would You Rather...

carry a big knife in the woods

carry an ax in the woods?

set up your own tent

find an empty abandoned tree house and sleep in it?

Would You Rather...

go to bed hungry

OR

go to bed angry?

go on a photo mission to get
great shots of gorilla

OR

go on a photo mission to
take a selfie with a seal?

Would You Rather...

be a grownup for a week

 OR

be a goldfish for a day?

go a year without candy

 OR

go a year without camping?

Would You Rather...

dance with a deer

sing with a swallow?

sleep on a pinecone

walk around with slippers
made of glass?

Would You Rather...

go camping in the Himalayas in Nepal

OR

go camping in the Fjords in Norway?

go camping in a 4X4 truck
to a rocky terrain

OR

go camping to a secluded
island beach in a boat?

Would You Rather...

get up early to see the sunrise

 OR

stay up late to see the sunset?

swing in a hammock

 OR

sip a hot mocha?

Would You Rather...

go camping in the Red
Deserts on Mars

OR

go camping on the Lunar
Highlands of the Moon?

drink hot cocoa in your tent

OR

drink water from a magic well that you
found in the middle of the forest?

Would You Rather...

roast marshmallows

OR

roast hotdogs?

play with rats

OR

be chased by cats?

Would You Rather...

go fishing

 OR

go diving?

pee in the shower

 OR

pee in the pool?

Would You Rather...

share candy with a raccoon

 OR

eat salad all afternoon?

be able to walk on water

 OR

be able to breathe underwater?

Would You Rather...

be off the grid while camping

 OR

stay in touch with family and friends?

camp with no food

 OR

camp with no water?

Would You Rather...

wake up and smell the roses

OR

wake up and smell the rain?

go camping for 2 weeks

OR

go camping for 2 nights?

Would You Rather...

play slack-lining

climb trees?

One last thing - we would love to hear
your feedback about this book!

If you found this activity book fun and useful, we
would be very grateful if you posted a short review on
Amazon! Your support does make a difference and we
read every review personally.

If you would like to leave a review, just head on
over to this book's Amazon page and click "Write a
customer review".

Thank you for your support!

Made in the USA
Monee, IL
03 May 2021